McCOMB PUBLIC LIBRARY
McCOMB, OHIO

D1473604

FAMOUS MOVIE MONSTERS™

MEET KING KONG

The Rosen Publishing Group, Inc.
New York

JAMES W. FISCUS

For Lenora Good, who has for many years helped find and fix problems in my manuscripts

Published in 2005 by The Rosen Publishing Group, Inc.
29 East 21st Street, New York, NY 10010

Copyright © 2005 by The Rosen Publishing Group, Inc.

First Edition

All rights reserved. No part of this book may be reproduced in any form without permission in writing from the publisher, except by a reviewer.

Library of Congress Cataloging-in-Publication Data

Fiscus, James W.
Meet King Kong/James W. Fiscus.
    p. cm.—(Famous movie monsters)
Includes bibliographical references and index.
ISBN 1-4042-0270-6 (library bdg.)
1. King Kong (Motion picture : 1933) I. Title. II. Series.
PN1997.K437F57 2005
791.43'72—dc22

2004010707

Manufactured in the United States of America

On the cover: In this still from *King Kong,* the mighty ape menaces those who try to stop him.

McCOMB PUBLIC LIBRARY
McCOMB, OHIO
NO. J05-217

CONTENTS

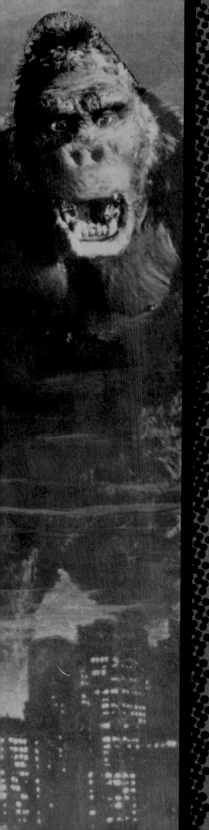

CHAPTER 1

THE STORY

The lights of New York City glow behind the city's docks as depression grips the country. Millions of people face hunger, and movie producer Carl Denham paces the captain's cabin on the freighter SS *Venture*. Frustration and anxiety gnaw at Denham. He has risked his future on his next film, but the ship carries enough ammunition to blow up the harbor and gas grenades that could knock out an elephant. If they do not sail by dawn, the *Venture* risks being held by the fire marshal. Delay would also mean facing monsoons in the Indian Ocean, where Denham plans to shoot his film, and he still does not have a leading lady. He charges ashore.

Hunger grips Ann Darrow as she paces the streets of the great city. Once an actress, Ann is one of millions of people without a job. Her hand reaches toward an apple, and the grocer clamps his hand on her arm. She faints from hunger as Denham stops the grocer from calling the police. Denham takes Ann to a restaurant, certain the pretty blonde is perfect for his movie. He enthusiastically asks her to star in the film. Ann knows who Denham is. At first afraid, she finally agrees to sail in the morning.

The *Venture* plows through the seas toward the Indian Ocean and a position Denham holds secret that is "way west of Sumatra." First mate Jack Driscoll slowly falls for Ann Darrow. He confronts the filmmaker and demands to know where they are going.

"I've never known it to fail: some big, hard-boiled egg gets a look at a pretty face and bang, he cracks up and goes sappy," Denham says. He pauses and adds, "It's the idea of my picture. The Beast was a tough guy, too. He could lick the world. But when he saw Beauty, she got him. He went soft. He forgot his wisdom and the little fellas licked him."

Later, Denham pulls out a map of their destination, Skull Island. A high wall guards the peninsula and its native village from the jungle beyond. "There's something on the other side

MAJOR CAST AND CREW
KING KONG (1933)

Executive producer: David O. Selznick
Directors/producers: Merian C. Cooper, Ernest B. Schoedsack (also camera operator)
Story by: Merian C. Cooper and Edgar Wallace
Screenplay by: James Ashmore Creelman and Ruth Rose
Original music by: Max Steiner
Chief technician: Willis H. O'Brien

MAIN CAST:

Fay Wray: Ann Darrow
Robert Armstrong: Carl Denham
Bruce Cabot: 1st Mate Jack Driscoll

WALK-ON CAST:

Merian C. Cooper: Pilot of the plane that kills Kong (uncredited)
Ernest B. Schoedsack: Machine gunner on the plane that kills Kong (uncredited)

The natives tie Ann Darrow (Fay Wray) to an altar to present her as a bride for Kong in a still from *King Kong*. The film went through several title changes during production, including *The Beast*, *The Ape*, *King Ape*, and *Kong*.

of it, something they fear," Denham says. "Kong!"

Reaching the coordinates on the map, the ship anchors at night as drums echo across the water. In the morning, the filmmakers see the great stone wall towering above palm trees. Skull Mountain rises into the sky. Ashore the next morning, they find the natives dancing and chanting, "Kong! Kong!" while hanging flowers on a native girl—the Bride of Kong! The chief demands Ann as a gift for Kong, and the crew retreats to the ship.

That night, Driscoll and Ann talk awkwardly of their mutual love. When the first mate is called to the captain's cabin, natives kidnap Ann. Taking rifles and gas grenades, Denham, Driscoll, Captain Englehorn, and crewmen pile into the *Venture*'s launch.

Ann struggles in terror as the natives drag her through a towering gate. Lashed to a high altar, Ann is left alone to face the night and the jungle. Torches wave from atop the wall. A great gong rings out as the chief calls Kong to his bride. Kong smashes trees from his path. The giant ape's anger vanishes when he sees Ann. Kong gently unties her. Ann faints as Kong carries her into the jungle.

Driscoll and Denham take half the crew and follow. Terror grips them as an armored dinosaur charges. The beast falls to a gas bomb and rifle fire, but soon a swamp blocks their way. Building a raft, they follow the sounds of Kong splashing

Kong menaces Driscoll and a group of sailors. *King Kong* originally contained a scene in which Kong shakes four sailors off the log. The sailors then fall into a ravine and are eaten alive by giant spiders. However, preview audiences were terrified by the scene, with some viewers actually leaving in the middle of the film. Merian C. Cooper decided to cut the scene, and the deleted clip has never been found.

Left: Kong crashes through the island gates as the natives attempt to shoot him. This set would later be used for the burning of Atlanta in *Gone with the Wind*. Above: Kong saves Ann from a hungry pteranodon. Willis O'Brien said the scene with Kong fighting the flying reptile was the hardest shot to film while making *King Kong*.

through the water. A brontosaurus (now called apatosaurus) rises from the fog and smashes the raft. The rescuers swim for their lives, but several are killed by the giant dinosaur. Hearing his pursuers, Kong puts Ann high in a dead tree and turns to attack. Kong finds Driscoll and a group of sailors crossing a log that has fallen over a deep ravine. He lifts the log and shakes it. Driscoll scrambles onto a ledge while the others fall to their deaths.

Kong turns back when Ann screams and rushes to challenge a hungry tyrannosaurus. Kong heroically fights the meat-eating dinosaur, finally breaking its jaw. He gently lifts Ann from the fallen tree and carries her up Skull Mountain to his lair. Denham, trapped on the village side of the ravine, turns back to get Captain Englehorn. Driscoll follows Kong.

Atop his mountain, Kong examines Ann. The giant ape is in love. A large flying reptile, a pteranodon, snatches Ann from the ledge. Kong again charges to the rescue. He grabs the pteranodon, forcing it to drop Ann. As Kong fights, Driscoll runs to Ann. With Ann holding on to him, Driscoll climbs over the edge of the high cliff and down a long vine. Killing the pteranodon, Kong pulls the pair toward him as they kick helplessly. As he is about to grab them, they let go and fall into the water far below.

They stagger back to the great wall, where Denham waits for a signal from Driscoll. Moments later, the warning gong rings over the village. Men rush to close the gate against Kong, who breaks down the massive doors. The sailors are saved only by Denham's gas bomb, which knocks out Kong. Denham orders the sailors to build a raft large enough to carry the ape.

Back in New York City, wealthy patrons file into a Broadway theater to see "King Kong—The Eighth Wonder of the World." Curtains open. Kong stands on a metal platform, chained to a massive metal cross. Kong watches silently as Denham brings Ann and Jack on stage. When reporters follow, Kong roars and struggles to break free. Flashbulbs fire as the reporters snap pictures. Kong snaps

Kong is presented as a Broadway attraction for New York theatergoers just moments before tearing off his chains and terrifying the audience. To produce a formidable wail for Kong, the filmmakers combined a lion's and a tiger's roar and ran the sound backward.

the chains holding his wrists. Everyone flees as Kong tears off the rest of his chains.

Ann and Driscoll seek shelter in a hotel across the street. Kong uses the hotel windows like a ladder and climbs the building, stopping to peer into windows looking for Ann. Finally, Kong sees Ann and Driscoll, who think they are safe. Kong crashes his fist through the window, knocking Driscoll aside and grabbing Ann. He carries her away across the city.

Kong heads for the highest place in New York, the Empire State Building. Hoping to shoot Kong if he sets Ann down, four navy biplanes scramble from a nearby airfield as the sun rises. Kong reaches the top of the world's tallest building and clutches the dirigible mooring mast with one hand as he holds Ann in the other. Worried by the planes, Kong puts Ann down on a high ledge.

The planes dive, their machine guns blasting. Again and again the aircraft strike. Leaning far out, Kong snags one plane and sends it crashing down. He weakens and staggers. Kong picks up Ann and looks at her in wonder and in pain. Gently, he sets her back on the ledge and strokes her a final time. Bullets rip into his throat. He tumbles to the ground, dwarfed by the great building, bouncing from ledge to ledge as he falls.

Driscoll scrambles up a ladder and helps Ann to safety.

Kong holds Ann in his giant clutches. Though Fay Wray shot to stardom in her role as Ann, she would never again achieve the same level of success in later films as she did with *King Kong*.

Kong terrorizes New York City from atop the Empire State Building. As *King Kong* was being shot, both the Empire State Building and the Chrysler Building were being constructed. At first, the filmmakers thought the Chrysler Building would end up being the taller of the two, and therefore the one Kong would climb. However, the Empire State Building wound up being the tallest, and so the script was changed midway through shooting.

On the street, Denham sadly approaches Kong's giant body. A police commander says, "Well, Denham, the airplanes got him."

"Oh, no," Denham says, "It wasn't the airplanes. It was Beauty killed the Beast."

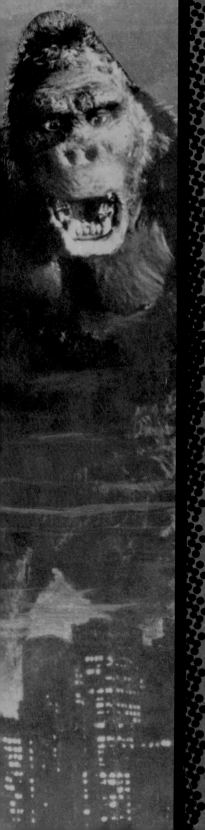

CHAPTER 2

THE MAKING OF KING KONG

The imagination of Merian C. Cooper, the special-effects genius of Willis O'Brien, and the skill and experience of Ernest Schoedsack drove the production of *King Kong*. O'Brien oversaw special effects. Schoedsack directed the live-action scenes. Cooper directed the technical scenes, such as Kong's life-size hand holding actress Fay Wray.

SCRIPTWRITING, CAST, AND PRODUCTION

King Kong was based on a story by mystery writer Edgar Wallace and ideas from Cooper. The first script of *King Kong*, written by Hollywood veteran James Ashmore Creelman, did not work for Cooper and Schoedsack. Cooper hired Ruth Rose to finish the job. While Rose had little scriptwriting experience, she had been on several of Cooper and Schoedsack's film expeditions and understood what they wanted.

Robert Armstrong (Carl Denham) was a stage actor who had made many silent and talking pictures before *King Kong*. Throughout his life, he remained a close friend to Schoedsack; Ruth Rose, who married Schoedsack in 1926; and Fay Wray. Fay Wray (Ann Darrow) came from Alberta, Canada. She had been in movies since 1923, when she was sixteen.

Jack Driscoll was the first role of Bruce Cabot's career. (His first released film was made between shootings for *King Kong*.) Cabot had worked as a seaman and in the oil-fields, and even as a sparring partner for a professional boxer. His *King Kong* screen test for Cooper involved climbing a rope hanging from a log bridge. Shooting *King Kong* was demanding work. Still photos of Wray and Cabot taken on the set between shots show how exhausted the actors often were.

Merian C. Cooper, pictured in a publicity shot from 1933, based his ideas for *King Kong* on his and Ernest Schoedsack's experiences traveling through exotic lands. Cooper and Schoedsack also played the pilot and the machine gunner on the plane that shoots down Kong.

The sound effects for the movie remain impressive, and the roars of Kong and various dinosaurs were used in a number of later films. Fay Wray's famous scream was also recycled for *The Son of Kong* (1933) and some other films. Veteran movie composer Max Steiner composed the score, or music, for *King Kong*. The score matches the high adventure of the film and is great fun by itself.

Shooting took more than a year. Back then, movies were often shot in a few days or weeks, so the shoot for *King Kong* was extremely long. Old sets on the RKO-Pathe film lot were altered and recycled to save time and money. A lavish set used to represent Jerusalem in the 1926 biblical epic *The King of Kings* became the great wall and gate in *King Kong*. Grass huts in a Polynesian village built for *Bird of Paradise* (1932) were moved to the old Jerusalem set. They became part of the Skull Island village. The sets were used in many other pictures in later years. Repainted, the wall was destroyed for the burning of Atlanta in *Gone with the Wind* (1939).

JOINT PRODUCTIONS OF JUNGLE EPICS

King Kong was filmed at the same time as another jungle adventure directed by Ernest Schoedsack, entitled *The Most Dangerous Game*. Robert Armstrong and Fay Wray played leading roles in both pictures. While that gave them the opportunity to work on *Game* during delays in shooting *King Kong*, it also complicated shooting. Often while Schoedsack was filming *Game*, Cooper and his crew would hang around the jungle set waiting to jump in and film scenes for *King Kong* during breaks. Cooper also frequently borrowed the stars of his film from the shooting of *Game*, sometimes delaying Schoedsack's work. As an added complication, Wray was a brunette (and played one in *Game*) but wore a blonde wig for *King Kong*. The wig kept slipping during the long, complex shots needed to merge her image with that of the model sets and animals used in *King Kong*.

The cast and crew film a scene set on Skull Island. Old sets from RKO films such as *The King of Kings* (1926) and *Bird of Paradise* (1932) were used for the Skull Island scenes to save money. Even so, the budget for *King Kong* was $650,000, a huge sum for a movie in those days.

WILLIS O'BRIEN AND STOP-MOTION ANIMATION

Chief technician Willis O'Brien used stop-motion animation and rear screen projection to turn small models into movie monsters and the landscapes they rampaged through. Moving-picture cameras take twenty-four individual still pictures, called frames, every second. When the film is projected, the images merge into the moving pictures we watch. Stop-motion animation involves photographing small models against a miniature set or a blank backdrop. The model is set in position and a single frame is exposed. The model is then moved slightly, and another frame is shot. The process is repeated again and again. When the final film is projected, the model appears to move.

The models of Kong were often photographed on a miniature set with small plants and trees. To avoid movement during the long days of shooting, the trees were often made of metal. Live plants were also used, creating problems. On one miniature set, a primrose simulated a large jungle plant. The crew shot frame by frame for an entire day. When they saw the film the next day, they realized that a primrose flower had bloomed. The stop-motion animation showed the white flower opening in seconds, huge against the miniature set. The scene had to be reshot.

At other times, Kong or the actors were photographed against a rear-projection screen. A projector behind a large screen projected an image on the screen. When models or actors were photographed in front of the screen, the projected image appeared to be scenery behind them. Shooting *King Kong*, Schoedsack pioneered a technique that later became common. For a scene in which the rescuers pass the twitching tail of a dying stegosaurus, he had the actors walk on a treadmill in front of a rear-projection screen. The projected scene showed the twitching tail of the stegosaurus, which had been filmed earlier. When the actors were filmed in front of the projected action, they appeared to be walking past the dinosaur.

O'Brien and his people also used glass mattes. Images were painted on a sheet of glass that was placed in front of the camera, which captured both the image on the matte and the scene beyond it. The mattes also allowed the filmmakers to expose film twice or more, with successive mattes blocking out parts of the shot. One matte might be clear in the center while the next would be blacked out in the center to allow exposure at the edges. Colored backdrops and filters were also used to make actors or models appear on film against an empty background. Those images could then be combined with other footage to put an actor in a miniature setting.

A model of Kong stands atop a mountain holding a miniature Fay Wray doll. Technician Willis O'Brien and director Ernest Schoedsack used stop-motion animation and rear screen projection to make models appear as full-size monsters.

O'Brien used several 18-inch-high (46-centimeter-high) models of Kong that were built to match sets on which 1 inch (2.5 cm) equals 1 foot (30.5 cm). The Kong models were built on metal skeletons with ball-and-socket joints that allowed full movement of the finished model. The skeleton, called an armature, was padded with foam rubber and

Special-effects wizard Ray Harryhausen, who worked with Willis O'Brien on *Mighty Joe Young* (1949), is shown in a 1994 photograph with one of the models used for *King Kong*. After O'Brien, Harryhausen became the next great master of stop-motion animation, working on such films as *Jason and the Argonauts* (1963) and *Clash of the Titans* (1981).

cotton and covered with rabbit skins to simulate Kong's fur. O'Brien and Cooper also used a life-size bust of Kong and a life-size hand to hold Fay Wray. They also built a life-size foot to trample Kong's victims. The full-size head had eyes that were 12 inches (30.5 cm) across, teeth 4 inches (10.1 cm) high, ears 1 foot (.30 m) high, and a 6-foot-wide (1.8 m) mouth that could grimace or smile. The nose was 2 feet (0.6 m) across and could twitch while the nostrils dilated as Kong breathed. The giant Kong could also "wag" his eyebrows.

The size of Kong varied in the film. He measured about 18 feet (5.5 m) tall while in the jungles on Skull Island, but against the towering buildings of Manhattan, he looked like a fly climbing a building. Cooper demanded that Kong always look gigantic. In much of the New York footage, the scale was adjusted to make Kong look 24 feet (7.3 m) tall.

When you watch the movie, you notice that Kong's fur appears to move as his muscles move. Kong's shimmering fur makes him truly come alive. The effect was an accident. Every time Willis O'Brien or another technician moved the models of Kong between shots, their fingers moved the rabbit fur that covered them. The resulting movement of Kong's fur was a surprising benefit. In addition, Kong's gestures and expressions always seem real. Kong's gestures were those of O'Brien, according to Orville Goldner and George Turner, who cite people who knew O'Brien in their book, *The Making of King Kong*.

After the film had been edited, Cooper felt it was too short and decided to shoot another sequence. The new scenes show Kong's attack on the elevated railroad in New York. They used "the most elaborate miniature sets" built for Kong, report Goldner and Turner. Technicians built a detailed set of the elevated streetcar tracks and trains and the area around them. Business signs and posters recorded the names of crew members: "Goldner's Chocolates," the "Delgado Building," "Gibson and Company," and others. One tiny poster advertised the opening of Cooper and Schoedsack's earlier documentary film *Chang: A Drama of the Wilderness*

(1927). A full-scale model of a train car was used to shoot scenes of passengers—extras and stuntmen and stuntwomen—tumbling and falling as the train crashes.

THE FILM'S BUDGET

The budget for *King Kong* was huge for its day. A "respectable 'A' feature could be brought in for $200,000," according to Goldner and Turner. *King Kong* cost $650,000. (Converting the film's 1932–1933 budget into modern dollars is complicated. Several conversion factors can be used, and there have been many changes in the movie business that increase the costs of production. However, when the 1933 *King Kong* is compared with recent blockbuster movies, there is no question that its budget would have been more than $100 million.) Money was saved by including many elements from an earlier production at RKO directed by Willis O'Brien. O'Brien's film *Creation* was filled with dinosaurs. When *Creation* was canceled, much of the development work and many of the models and sets were used in *King Kong*, saving $230,000.

A splashy poster for *King Kong* showcases the terrifying ape. The film was a box-office sensation, grossing $90,000 in its first four days, the biggest opening ever at the time.

CHAPTER 3

THE ORIGINS OF KING KONG

One of the greatest adventure films of all time flickered onto America's movie screens in 1933, bringing adventure and thrills to a nation mired in the Great Depression. Motion pictures were new. Full-length movies had told grand stories for barely twenty years. The movies had sound for scarcely five years. All movies were filmed in black and white. It would be nearly three decades before television dominated American homes. Even radio was just getting started as Americans' major link to the world outside their homes.

King Kong was made during the first great era of talking movies, a time of thrilling adventure movies. People flocked to *Dracula* (1931) to watch Bela Lugosi's hypnotic eyes. Boris Karloff terrified audiences in *Frankenstein* (1931) and *The Mummy* (1932). Tarzan's famous yell first echoed through the jungle in a movie with sound the year before *King Kong*'s release.

To mark the fiftieth anniversary of *King Kong* in 1983, a giant inflatable Kong was hung from the Empire State Building in New York City. Once again, the monstrous ape

In 1983, in honor of the fiftieth anniversary of *King Kong*, an inflatable Kong was hoisted above the Empire State Building. The film was so popular that it was released four times between 1933 and 1952 and was named one of the 100 best films of all time by the National Film Registry of the Library of Congress.

appeared to climb the towering building. *King Kong* came from our legends of giants and monsters and from the lives of the people who created the movie.

THE INFLUENCE OF EARLY EPICS AND ADVENTURES

One of the earliest adventure stories, an epic poem from ancient Greece called the *Odyssey*, tells of the struggles of the Greek hero Odysseus to return home after the Trojan War. Odysseus and his crew steal food from a Cyclops (the Cyclopes were giants with only one eye), and the giant eats several of them in revenge. Odysseus blinds the Cyclops and escapes. The Cyclops, however, is both sympathetic and monstrous. The same can be said about many other mythical monsters. Humans have feared them even as they sympathize with them, as we do with Kong when he enters a world he cannot understand.

Rumors of large apes reached Western civilization 2,500 years ago when a sailor from Carthage named Hanno fought them in what is now Sierra Leone. (Hanno may have encountered chimpanzees, baboons, or even lowland gorillas.) Not until the late 1840s did Europeans clearly describe gorillas. Soon, reports of adventurers in Africa were filled with tales of half-ape, half-human monsters.

Books and movies soon combined to spread stories of lost worlds and hidden wonders. Edgar Allan Poe made a monstrous ape the killer in his 1841 story *The Murders in the Rue Morgue*, which was made into films in 1914 and 1932. Starting in 1912, Edgar Rice Burroughs turned out *Tarzan of the Apes* and the many Tarzan books that followed. (*Tarzan* was first filmed in 1918.) *Tarzan* was preceded by the African adventure novels of H. Rider Haggard—*King Solomon's Mines, Allan Quatermain*, and *She*—all of which were written in the 1880s. *She* was filmed six times before the release of *King Kong*. Perhaps the most important book and movie combination for the origins of *King Kong* was written by Sir Arthur Conan Doyle, the creator of the detective Sherlock Holmes. In

This still from *The Lost World* (1925) shows a brontosaurus terrorizing Londoners outside the Bank of England. Willis O'Brien's special-effects work on this film would influence the techniques he used for later films such as *King Kong.*

1912, he published a novel of grand adventure, *The Lost World*, which tells of an expedition to a plateau deep in the jungles where primitive tribes fight dinosaurs to survive. Willis O'Brien's 1925 film of *The Lost World* helped him develop many of the special-effects techniques he would later use in making *King Kong*. Thus, ancient stories, modern books, and the new movie industry all contributed to the origin of *King Kong*.

THE REAL ADVENTURES BEHIND *KING KONG*

While *King Kong* comes from stories of unknown lands and monsters, it also comes from the adventures lived by three of its creators: Merian C. Cooper, Ernest Schoedsack, and Schoedsack's wife, screenwriter Ruth Rose.

During the 1920s, no one could turn on a TV set and see a dozen channels showing exotic people and places. Few Americans could spend months traveling with nomads in Iraq and Iran or sailing to Thailand to see tigers and stampeding elephants. Cooper and Schoedsack did so and brought movies back to Americans eager for adventure. When Cooper hired Ruth Rose to write *King Kong*, he told her, "Give it the spirit of a real Cooper-Schoedsack expedition." She did.

Both Cooper and Schoedsack served in the U.S. Army in France during World War I (1914–1918). Cooper flew for the Air Service while Schoedsack was a cameraman for the Signal Corps. The two men met in Vienna, Austria, early in 1919 and first collaborated during 1922 and 1923 when they filmed an expedition studying remote parts of the world. They traveled to Addis Ababa in Ethiopia, where Schoedsack filmed Ras (or Prince) Tafari Makonnen. (Ras Tafari changed his name to Haile Selassie when he became emperor.) Their Ethiopian films were lost when the ship they traveled on burned.

With their first film destroyed, they planned their next venture. Joined by American writer Marguerite Harrison, they traveled to Turkey. Their trip would result in one of the greatest documentary films ever made—*Grass: A Nation's Battle for Life* (1925). The Turks had just won a bloody war against Greece, Great Britain, and France, driving all three nations from Turkey. The filmmakers waited at Ankara (in a region of Turkey called Anatolia) for permission to travel farther east. They were dogged by Turkish intelligence agents who thought they were spies. Finally, they stopped waiting for permission and escaped south across the Tarsus Mountains into Iraq.

Reaching the Iranian province of Khuzestan at the northern end of the Persian Gulf, they joined the Bakhtiari people for their annual migration. The Bakhtiari spent the winter in the lowlands of Khuzestan next to southern Iraq. When the heat of summer killed the grass, they migrated across the rugged Zagros Mountains to their summer pastures in the highlands near the city of Isfahan. (Many of the Bakhtiari still make the migration.) The trio of moviemakers drank sheep's buttermilk and ate bread so hard that "Schoedsack damaged his revolver-butt while trying to break up a chunk," according to Goldner and Turner. Pictures of the tribes crossing a swift river on rafts made of inflated animal skins and zigzagging in a long, black line up the glacier are some of the most dramatic images ever filmed.

Released in 1925, *Grass* had a long, successful run in New York. While Cooper managed the company in New York, Schoedsack signed on as cinematographer with a New York Zoological Society expedition to the Sargasso Sea and the Galápagos Islands aboard the SS *Arcturus*. On the voyage, he met the expedition's historian and research technician, Ruth Rose.

Edward E. Rose, Ruth's father, was a producer, playwright, and actor in New York City. Ruth Rose was raised in the theater and had acted in a number of plays and films before volunteering to work at the Zoological Society's Tropical Research Station in British Guiana. She started by doing unskilled jobs but quickly became a full member of the research team, helping capture various animals, including a large boa constrictor. Because of her writing ability, she became the expedition's historian. Schoedsack and Ruth Rose grew close while on the *Arcturus* and married in 1926.

Cooper and Schoedsack traversed difficult terrain to film scenes such as this one for *Chang: A Drama of the Wilderness*. The film was a documentary about a Laotian family struggling to survive in the jungle and featured stunning shots of many wild, exotic animals that the directors risked their lives to capture on film.

When Schoedsack returned from the *Arcturus* trip, he and Cooper headed for the jungles of Thailand to make a second "natural drama," as they called their films. Far in the jungles of northeast Thailand, near the border with Laos, they filmed *Chang: A Drama of the Wilderness*. To reach their destination, they started from Bangkok by train, then traveled by horse, foot, and log canoe. The pair crossed mountains, dozens of rivers, and hundreds of miles of jungle.

They filmed a Laotian family surviving in the jungle. Laotian houses were built on high platforms so that the family would be safe from animals and floods. Schoedsack was accused by later writers of using trick photography to take his stunning shots of animals, but he did not. He also used a standard lens, not a telephoto lens, which would have allowed him to keep his distance from the animals. Cooper stood by with his rifle as Schoedsack filmed, saving him from likely death several times. For one shot, Schoedsack built a platform high in a tree and lay filming downward as a tiger clawed its way up the tree toward him. The tiger's head fills the screen.

The most dramatic sequence in *Chang* (the Lao word for "elephant") is of elephants stampeding through a village. Schoedsack dug a pit seven feet deep and covered it with heavy timbers. He built a low turret in the center of the roof, allowing him to film at ground level as the elephants charged over his head. One of the elephants turned back and put his foot through the camera turret. Schoedsack ducked from the pieces of shattered logs. *Chang* proved a great success when it opened in New York in 1927.

The next project for Cooper-Schoedsack Productions was an adventure set in Africa, *The Four Feathers* (1929). They filmed the animal scenes in East Africa, in what is now Tanzania. Ruth Rose (now married to Ernest Schoedsack) managed the accounts, doctored the staff, and stood guard with a rifle when necessary. The team brought back films of a hippopotamus stampede over a riverbank (the hippos did not want to cooperate for the camera) and a troop of baboons, as well as of other animals. The African footage was edited together with film of actors shot in California.

Cooper and the Schoedsacks knew the jungle and knew adventure. When Rose wrote the character of Ann Darrow, a woman willing to sail across the oceans on a great adventure, she wrote of a life she had lived. When the character of filmmaker Carl Denham explains that he always worked his own camera because once when he was filming in Africa his cameraman panicked, he says, "I'd have got a swell picture of a charging rhino but the cameraman got scared. The darned fool! I was right there with a rifle. Seems he didn't trust me to get the rhino before it got him. I haven't fooled with cameramen since, I do it myself." Cooper and the Schoedsacks had done it themselves.

CHAPTER 4

THE PHENOMENON OF KING KONG

RKO-Pathe Pictures, the studio that made *King Kong*, was in deep financial trouble when production started. *Kong*'s large budget was a huge risk for RKO. If *King Kong* failed to bring people into theaters, the studio might go out of business.

King Kong opened in New York City on March 2, 1933, with its national release a month later. For the first time, a movie premiered in the two largest theaters in the country, Radio City Music Hall and the RKO Roxy. *King Kong* made $90,000 (or about $3,800,000 in 2003, based on the average wage of workers) in its first four days, at a time when tickets cost an average of about 15¢. *King Kong* set box-office records. During its first week in New York, at only the two theaters, an estimated 150,000 people saw the film. The Roxy had opened in 1927 and was in financial trouble. The profits from *Kong* saved the theater, which was not torn down until 1960. The profits from *King Kong* also saved RKO-Pathe Pictures.

The movie was censored to conform to Hollywood's new, and infamous, production code and rereleased in 1938 because some scenes were considered too graphic. The cut scenes included:

- shots of the brontosaurus chewing on two sailors, so it killed only three men instead of five;

- part of the scene where Kong strips off Ann's dress and sniffs it;

- shots of Kong attacking the Skull Island village, biting and chewing natives, stomping one into the mud, and knocking over a tower; and

- two scenes in New York City, one of Kong chewing on a man in the street and the scene in which Kong pulls a woman from her hotel room and drops her to her death after determining that she is not Ann.

The censored scenes were restored in the 1970s and can be seen in the sixtieth anniversary VHS tape. (A fully restored *King Kong* DVD is expected to be released in 2005 to take advantage of the release of Peter Jackson's new version of the film.)

The 1938 run of *King Kong* became the first time that a feature movie was rereleased as a first-run film. It again made huge profits for RKO. When *King Kong* was released yet again in 1952, it brought in "two-and-a-half times the gross expected of a new 'A' release," according to Goldner and Turner. *Time* magazine named the 1952 rerelease

Movie of the Year. With the rise of television in the 1950s, *King Kong* was broadcast often and remained a favorite with TV viewers.

One of the most famous stories about *King Kong* involves a scene that does not appear in the movie. Before its general release, *King Kong* contained a scene showing sailors falling from the log bridge into a ravine filled with giant spiders and scorpions. The monsters attack the men. In the same test reel, a giant spider rather than a lizard climbs the vine to attack Driscoll. The scene was in the film when it was previewed, but in the words of Merian Cooper, "It stopped the picture cold, so the next day back at the studio, I took it out myself." Several of the spider and insect models survive along with a few still photographs. O'Brien used several of the monsters in a later film, entitled *The Black Scorpion* (1957).

Movie critics generally loved *King Kong*. The Academy Awards did not, and the movie failed to earn even one nomination for an award. But in the end, *King Kong* won: few people remember the Best Picture winner for 1933—*Cavalcade*—and the National Film Registry of the Library of Congress has placed *King Kong* on its list of the 100 greatest films.

King Kong is a cultural icon. He has been featured in political cartoons, greeting cards, music videos, and on a wide variety of advertisements. The giant ape has pitched rum, bras, management companies, and thrill rides at amusement parks. He has graced the covers of *Mad*, *National Lampoon*, *Esquire*, and comic books. Kong's influence can even be seen in episodes of the cartoon series *South Park*.

The team behind *King Kong* reunited to make *Mighty Joe Young* in 1949. The film tells the story of an ape that is raised in Africa by a young girl (Terry Moore, *above*) and brought to America as a nightclub attraction. The movie was a success and earned Willis O'Brien the first Oscar for special effects.

REMAKES AND SPIN-OFFS

Almost immediately after the opening of *King Kong*, work began on a sequel. Released later in 1933, *The Son of Kong* came from the production team responsible for *King Kong*. Cooper and Schoedsack produced and directed, Ruth Rose wrote the story and screenplay, Willis O'Brien served as chief technician, and Max Steiner wrote the score. *The Son of Kong* also brought back Robert Armstrong as producer Carl Denham. Several other original cast members also returned for the new film. Fay Wray's scream became the scream of *The Son of Kong* actress Helen Mack.

RKO allowed only $250,000 to make *The Son of Kong*. Ruth Rose said, "If you can't make it bigger, you'd better make it funnier," according to Goldner and Turner. She kept the film light. Although *The Son of Kong* does not have the spectacle of *King Kong*, the characterizations are better. The younger ape, Kong Jr., is more expressive and sympathetic than the senior ape. The movie is great fun.

The next real incarnation of a giant ape in the movies came in 1949, when the main team from *King Kong* made *Mighty Joe Young*. Cooper produced and created the story. Ruth Rose wrote the screenplay, and Schoedsack directed. Willis O'Brien won a special Academy Award for *Joe*, the first Oscar for special effects. *Mighty Joe Young* is a lot of fun, telling of a large ape raised in Africa by a beautiful girl (Terry Moore) and brought to America for a nightclub show.

Mighty Joe Young links O'Brien with the next great master of stop-motion animation, Ray Harryhausen. Harryhausen's films made over the next three and a half decades included the most stunning stop-motion animation ever filmed (including *Jason and the Argonauts* [1963] and *Clash of the Titans* [1981]). *Mighty Joe Young* was remade in 1998.

In 1976, Italian producer Dino De Laurentiis released his take on Kong. Despite massive publicity about models of the giant ape and how closely the film would follow the original, it fell flat. De Laurentiis moved the action from the 1930s to the

The 1976 remake of *King Kong*, directed by John Guillermin, had Kong climbing the Twin Towers in the final scene rather than the Empire State Building. Though the film was a critical disappointment, it made enough money to warrant a sequel, *King Kong Lives* (1986).

modern day and gave his movie a harsh edge. The character of Ann Darrow, for example, was changed from a woman voluntarily willing to face danger into a failed party girl named Dwan, who is found adrift in a lifeboat. Carl Denham became a greedy oilman rather than an adventurous filmmaker. The film made enough money to generate a sequel in 1986, *King Kong Lives*, which lost a great deal of money.

The giant apes have appeared in many lesser movies. Kong himself fought the Japanese monster Godzilla in 1962. Movies titled *Konga* (1961), *APE* (1976), and *Queen Kong* (1977) have come and gone quickly. Kong even starred in an animated cartoon on television in 1966.

ACADEMIC AND SOCIAL CRITICS DISSECT *KING KONG*

Academic and social critics have read great significance into *King Kong*. The movie's view of the natives of Skull Island reflects the colonialist attitudes of the time. According to some critics, *King Kong* is thus a racist expression of the stereotypes believed by white Americans and Europeans in the 1920s and 1930s. Reversing the charge of racism,

THE NEXT KONG

The next version of *King Kong* will come from director Peter Jackson. Jackson's three films of J. R. R. Tolkien's *Lord of the Rings* were an enormous artistic, critical, and box-office success. The same writing and production team that Jackson commanded when he made the *Lord of the Rings* trilogy is working with him on his version of *King Kong*. As he did in *Lord of the Rings*, Jackson will film in New Zealand.

According to Universal Studios, the film will be set at the same time as the original. More time will be spent on Skull Island than in the original, however. Jackson has cast his three leads. Comic actor Jack Black will play Carl Denham, while Oscar winner Adrien Brody is set to play Jack Driscoll. Australian actress Naomi Watts will play Ann Darrow. The film is scheduled for release late in 2005.

some writers see Kong as a black hero brought in chains to America where he is killed when he rebels.

Feminist writers have also analyzed the movie. Some see Ann Darrow as a liberated woman willing to face danger for the sake of adventure. Others see her as a Victorian heroine, spending her time alternately screaming in terror or fainting.

Finally, socialists and communists have seen Kong as a hero of the working class. When the great ape breaks down the massive gate on Skull Island, he is striking at the political and economic elite. He is doing it again when he destroys the symbols of the power structure in New York.

Goldner and Turner concisely answer the writers who have heavily analyzed *King Kong*:

> . . . the simple explanations are best: Kong was not darker in hue than any other gorilla, he smashed open the gates solely because he wanted to recapture Fay Wray, his atrocious behavior in the city had nothing to do with politics or economic conditions and he climbed the Empire State Building because it was the highest point in the city, corresponding to his mountain-top lair in his homeland. *King Kong* is exactly what it was meant to be: A highly entertaining, shrewdly conceived work of pure cinema.

FILMOGRAPHY

Note: Availability of films on VHS tape or DVD is based on information posted on the Web site http://www.imdb.com.

THE GOOD APES

King Kong (1933). On VHS and DVD. Directors: Merian C. Cooper and Ernest B. Schoedsack. The original Kong and still the best big ape on film.

Mighty Joe Young (1949). On VHS. Director: Ernest B. Schoedsack. Jill Young raises the large ape, Joe, in Africa and later brings him to America. A well-done, fun film.

Son of Kong, The (1933). On VHS. Director: Ernest B. Schoedsack. Fun sequel to *King Kong*, with Carl Denham returning to Skull Island and finding Kong's son.

REMAKES AND LESSER APES

King Kong (1976). On VHS and DVD. Director: John Guillermin. Producer: Dino De Laurentiis. Extensive remake of *King Kong* that puts a harsh, petty twist on the original. Models and an actor in an ape suit were used to create Kong.

King Kong (2005). In production. Director: Peter Jackson.

King Kong Lives (1986). On VHS. Director: John Guillermin. Producer: Dino De Laurentiis. Sequel to De Laurentiis's

1976 remake of *King Kong*; the film lost massive
amounts of money.

Mighty Joe Young (1998). On VHS and DVD. Director: Ron
Underwood. Remake of 1949 film has good computerized
effects but misses the mark, despite efforts of future
Oscar-winner Charlize Theron as Jill Young.

RANDOM APES

King Kong Vs. Godzilla (1962). On VHS and DVD. Director:
Ishirô Honda. Clash of giant monsters inspired by an
idea lifted from Willis O'Brien. Standard Japanese monster
movie with actors wearing lizard and ape suits.

Konga (1961). Also called *I Was a Teenage Gorilla*. On VHS.
Director: John Lemont. British movie about an evil scientist
who learns how to force growth in plants and animals. He
turns a baby chimpanzee into a monster ape that rampages
through London.

Mighty Kong, The (1998). On VHS. Director: Art Scott. Animated
(cartoon) version of *King Kong*, done as a musical.

GLOSSARY

editing The process of removing unwanted film footage while combining other footage to produce the final movie.

matte An object used to block part of a camera's field of view.

model A smaller version of a large creature or object.

rear screen projection Special-effect technique in which a film or still picture is projected from the rear against a large screen. When actors or models are photographed in front of the screen, the projected image appears to be the background behind them.

screenplay The script containing the dialogue and instructions for the actors in a movie.

silent movies Movies made without spoken dialogue.

stop-motion animation Special-effect technique in which a model is photographed on a single frame of movie film, moved, and photographed in a process that is repeated twenty-four times to produce one second of the final moving picture. When the film is projected, the images merge into the moving pictures we watch.

FOR MORE INFORMATION

American Film Institute
2021 North Western Avenue
Los Angeles, CA 90027-1657
(323) 856-7600
Web site: http://www.afi.com

The Fay Wray Pages
http://www.shillpages.com/faywray/fwmain.shtml
This site has many photographs from *King Kong*.

Internet Movie Database
http://www.imdb.com
This site allows you to search movies by title, person, character, and other criteria.

King Kong—The Eighth Wonder of the World!
http://www.aboyd.com/Kong/index2.html
Large site dedicated to *King Kong*.

WEB SITES

Due to the changing nature of Internet links, the Rosen Publishing Group, Inc., has developed an online list of Web sites related to the subject of this book. This site is updated regularly. Please use this link to access the list:

http://www.rosenlinks.com/famm/mekk

FOR FURTHER READING AND VIEWING

Chang: A Drama of the Wilderness (1927). Available on VHS and DVD. Cooper and Schoedsack's second documentary film, made in northern Thailand. Spectacular shots of tigers, elephants, and other animals and of the lives of the Laotian villagers.

Grass: A Nation's Battle for Life (1925). Available on VHS and DVD. Cooper and Schoedsack's first documentary film shows the grueling migration of Iran's Bakhtiari tribes as they move from dry winter pastures to green summer grass. The film has stunning pictures of the Bakhtiari crossing swift rivers on inflated goatskins and climbing up the long, brutal slopes of the mountains that block their path.

Haining, Peter, ed. *Movie Monsters: Great Horror Film Stories.* New York: Severn House, 1988. Retelling of classic monster stories or copies of the original stories. Includes "Prologue: Inviting Frankenstein into the Parlour" by Ray Bradbury, "Balaoo, the Demon Baboon" by G. Leroux, "The Golem" by C. Bloch, "The Beetle" by R. Marsh, "The Mummy" by Arthur Conan Doyle, "King Kong" by Edgar Wallace and D. M. Dell, "The Bride of Frankenstein" by Mary Shelley and G. Preston, "Dracula's

Daughter" by Bram Stoker, "The War of the Worlds" by H. G. Wells, "The Beast from 20,000 Fathoms" by Ray Bradbury, "The Night of the Demon" by M. R. James, "The Fly" by G. Langelaan, and "The Thing" by John W. Campbell Jr.

Lost World, The (1925). Available on VHS and DVD. Directed by Harry O. Hoyt. Willis H. O'Brien, technical director. O'Brien used this film to refine many of the special-effects techniques he would later use when making *King Kong*.

Steiner, Max. *King Kong* original 1933 motion picture score. Southern Cross Records, 1976. Southern Cross Records: SCCD 901. Compact disc.

Trader Horn (1931). Available on VHS. Directed by W. S. Van Dyke. Early African adventure film with some of the most spectacular animal photography of any Hollywood film.

BIBLIOGRAPHY

Bahrenburg, Bruce. *The Creation of Dino De Laurentiis' King Kong*. New York: Pocket Books, 1976.

Erb, Cynthia. *Tracking King Kong: A Hollywood Icon in World Culture*. Detroit: Wayne State University Press, 1998.

Goldner, Orville, and George E. Turner. *The Making of* King Kong: *The Story Behind a Film Classic.* New York: A. S. Barnes and Company, 1975.

Gottesman, Ronald, and Harry M. Geduld. *The Girl in the Hairy Paw: King Kong as Myth, Movie, and Monster.* New York: Avon Books/Flare, 1976.

Pascall, Jeremy. *The King Kong Story.* Secaucus, NJ: Chartwell Books, 1977.

INDEX

ABOUT THE AUTHOR

James W. Fiscus is a Portland, Oregon, writer and historian. He has a master's degree in Middle East and Asian history and taught military history at Portland State University. Before obtaining his MA degree, he worked as a photojournalist in Portland. He served in the U.S. Navy in Vietnam. In addition to writing about history, he reports on medicine, science, business, and law for numerous publications. He also publishes fiction and has been a movie fan for most of his life.

PHOTO CREDITS

Cover, p. 1 © Sunset Boulevard/Corbis Sygma; p. 1 illustration by Thomas Forget; pp. 4, 9, 11, 13, 14, 23, 24, 32 © Bettmann/Corbis; pp. 6, 7, 12, 17, 19, 37 © Hulton/Archive/Getty Images, Inc.; p. 8 © Underwood and Underwood/Corbis; pp. 15, 29 © The Everett Collection; p. 20 © Rufus F. Folkks/Corbis; p. 22 © Swim Ink/Corbis; p. 26 © John Springer Collection/Corbis; p. 35 © Corbis Sygma.

Designer: Thomas Forget; Editor: Kathy Kuhtz Campbell